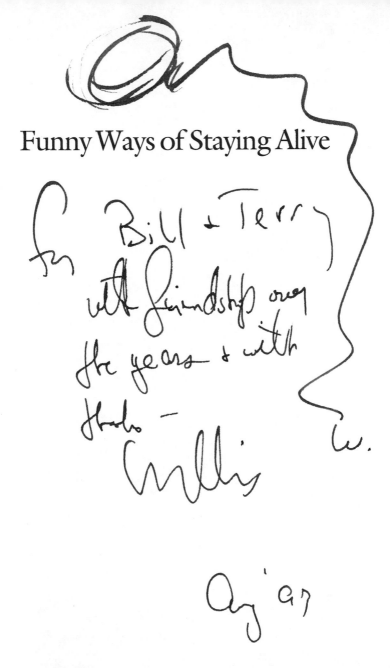

Funny Ways of Staying Alive

For Bill & Terry
with friendship over
the years & with
thanks —

W.

Aug '97

Funny Ways of Staying Alive

❖

Willis Barnstone

University Press of New England

Hanover and London

For

Beatrice Kammerman

and

Chou Ping

University Press of
New England
Hanover, NH 03755
© 1993 by
University Press of
New England
5 4 3 2 1
CIP data appear at the
end of the book

Contents

Ways of Darkness

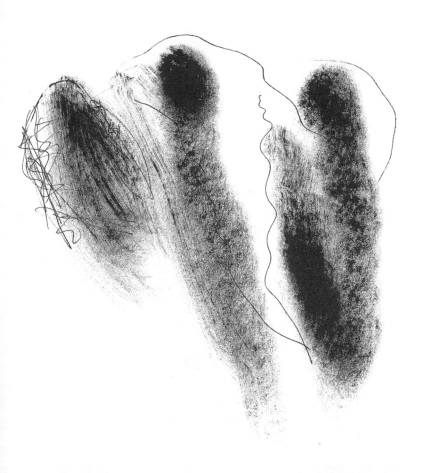

Sometimes in solitude,

The truth is rude.

Smoke

And croak.

Croak, croak,

The world is a joke.

Grin

At the darkness we are in.

The mole
Is digging for its soul.

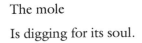

The hunger shark
Is singing in the dark.

Over the wheat the autumn crows
Blackly ignore the rose.

You are grave and even in sleep

Grow deep.

Awake you puff and sound

Profound.

Then dropping pompously down to the floor
     of your soul,

You pop out a dark and deadly hole.

To feel the naked truth,

Undress and pull your tooth.

Is it possible
To know an unseen daffodil?

In Somalia a child dies anonymously.
A drop is nameless in the sea.

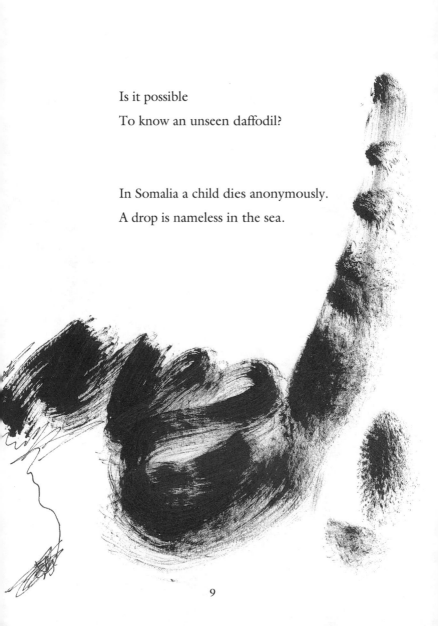

When a pal lets you drown,
You feel let down.

How easy
To be sleazy!

Don't be fickle
To a friend in a pickle.

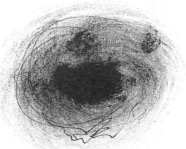

A man with a gun
Is a barrel of fun.

Don't trifle
With a rifle.

Love the bomb
And lose your mom.

11

A man unshaven
Looks like a raven.

If you hurry when you shave,
Your blood will rave.

If you have to run,
Move slowly like the sun.

After many a drink
You stink.

Fried and drive?
Wanted Dead or Alive.

A slaphappy drunk
At the wheel is a murdering punk.

When you bravely stumble
In a somber alien jungle.
A laughing lion may see fit
To chew you out a bit.

When you smooch and huddle
In a puddle,
The long watery kisses you won't forget.
Though your feet are wet.

If you chat a lot
In a Dead Sea cave with the wife of Lot,
It's not your fault
But you smell of salt.

Change your socks
Or smell of lox.

If you hate death,
Don't hold your breath.

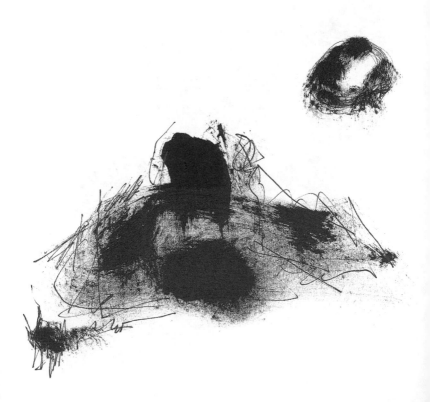

Comes the rat. Worry and seethe
Or cool it and breathe.

Earth is a mythic park
Of birth, a quick day and night
Of light,
And underground a huge ash-and-bone tree
Growing eternally
From endless dying into the dark.

The heart bashed and untuned

Can't hide.

It clonks grimly outside,

A mess

On your dress.

You wear it like a bloody wound.

Slow bright time

Is a rhyme

For life.

The race horse sings,

Time's spinning hand cures our ills

And, on halting,

Time's knife

Of darkness kills.

The ways
Of darkness go from mud to daybreak haze.

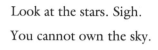

Look at the stars. Sigh.
You cannot own the sky.

Since Blake saw angels in a tree,

Why not seek fire under the sea?

Ways of Stress

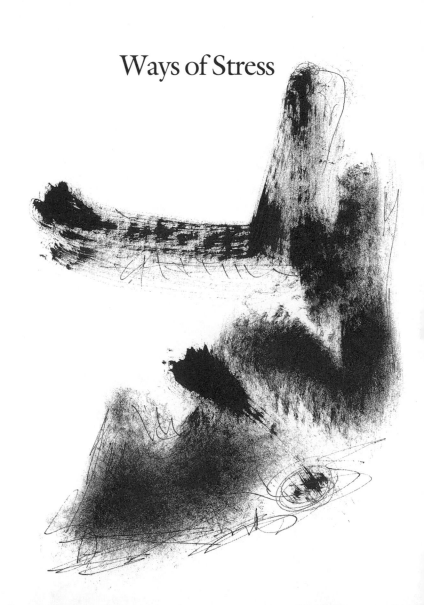

When you lose your keys,
Your options freeze.

When a lawyer phones hello,
You've lost a pile of dough.

When a dentist drills,
Think of daffodils.

When a doctor kills,
Change pills.

It's nice to chat with a mechanic
Who's not satanic.

A summer with a plumber
Is a bummer.

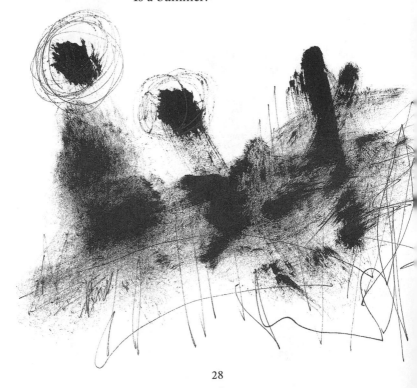

When your spouse is a louse,
Don't be a mouse.

If sex is stress,
Don't undress.

A wild dog who steals for more
Is always poor.

Rob

And sob.

Angry? Don't whine.

Go kick a porcupine.

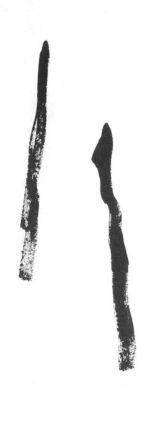

Out of your mind? Kick the universe
And break your foot or worse.

Spit at the sky.
Dry your eye.

Trap a nightingale.

Go to jail.

If your shoes are tight,
You're not so bright.

When you wear your boots to bed,
Your feet are in your head.

If someone calls for money,

It's funny?

Mumble.

Grumble.

Stumble.

If you conform,

Obeying the norm,

Slime

Is your crime

And your term

Is *worm*.

Are you a cranky dinosaur?

You could be a big bore.

If you're greedy,
You're always needy.

Don't insult a Pole or any other.

He may be your mother.

Poor reader,

I've been the feeder

Of this spree

Of misery.

But don't beef

About the soup of grief.

Why mope?

Just brush your teeth and elope

Into the arms of hope.

Ways of Hope

When you are young and unafraid,
Sing in the unknown shade.

God said, "This apple tree

Is all for me."

Despite the *NO* by the grand misanthrope,

Daring Eve ate

And gave us death, our birth, and hope.

Eve and her snitching mate

Would still be sharing an idyllic state

Of impotence in paradise

If Eve had not got wise.

Why
Be a wise guy?
It's cool
To risk and be a fool?

Play a saxophone on a star?
Dante sang in Paradiso
but didn't go
half that far.

One stormy tower

Is a man and woman in a shower.

Want some fun?

Tickle my bun.

When you need to pee
Nicest is the sea.

If you need fame
Change your name
To Einstein
And buy a brain.

What if you lose your hair?

Don't despair.

You win a magic touch

Since women love a baldy twice as much.

If you happen to leave on the light
Through the night,
You're working hard, you're dead,
Or having fun in bed.

When you eat

No red meat,

Your heart will dance

And singing lambs will prance.

Jog
And your heart won't clog.

Dream a verse
And swing on the universe.

Blocked?
Your pen locked?
Fart,
And start.

When you feel blue
Don't color up with a blue tattoo.

Doubt
And you're out.

Persist
And you exist.

If you don't care to hug
The mug
Of a polar bear in the snow,
Crawl into
A cozy igloo
And kiss an Eskimo.

Go to the Perigord
In France.
Eat truffle, drink *rouge*,
And wake in a trance.

If you would find the Tao,
Don't eat too much chow.

Go

To Mexico.

Lie down

On a carnation and lose your frown.

Tan

By the jaguar in ancient Yucatan

Or foxtrot

On a slow ox cart.

And while your rhyme may fail,

Your heart will sail.

If you seek a dark night

And dumb flight

Up to oblivion and timeless harmony,

Do nothing. Don't see.

Be.

If you like to dance, dance alone.

Don't groan

Or crack your bones

With grief. Forget, and hear

The orchard chanting in your ear.

A huge orange butterfly

Tugs the sky

And calmly thunders in your eye.

The way into your soul?
There is no hole.
You are a small tree
And inside grows a black sea.

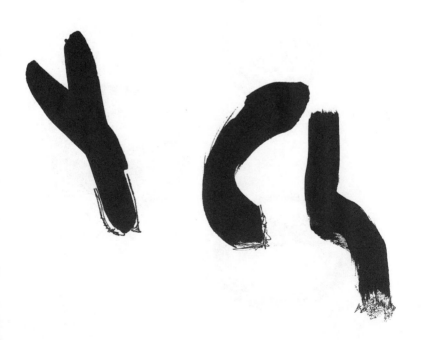

When you burn,
You learn.

Into his own labyrinth
Theseus takes a hyacinth
But finds that to unknot
Thought
A rope of pain is a guide
When lost inside.

From the inner dark,

Go outdoors for release

In stark

White Greece.

Adam ate an apple and was glib

With Eve. She lay nude and gutsy on a borrowed rib.

Adam got hot and jumped her. But the sap

Yelled murder. She took the rap.

Prometheus gave us fire. In one good night

Of love, Eve gave us light.

Ways of Death

Death when far is finitely clear
And infinitely far when near.

Tonight a brother's gone.

It's late to telephone

Or write words which before

Were mute. Ignore

The risk of love? Oh yes. We learn

Too late to turn

And look at sun inside the near tulip tree

Or in the heart's sea.

When a brother decides to die

You cry.

He left a note to say
He loves us all. High glory and hell were his way.
Now his unwise
Word is gentle and purifies.

Night has won.
What happened to the sun?

After the rites, tedium,

And you are numb.

After the grave

You save

A memory of genius and cruelty. Hold on

To love so all is not undone.

When your love lies in a pine box
Haunting your sleep, be like a fox.
Cunning. Escape
With him to chat inside a lucid grape.

A plain pine box in the mind
Lingers behind.
You miss someone. He left early. Then
The sun rises again.

Be still. Be still.

Lose your will.

When evening comes the shadowed face

Of mountains won't erase

One

Cold dream of sun.

Ways of Poets

Lorca in the lemon spring
Of Andalusia. Bury him in spear-
mint or a weather vane.
Then shed only one tear
Of pain
And blood over his moon,
And let him sing.

Antonio Machado in the cold fall
Of Soria walks by his old elm. Recall,
As he did,
How a young wife changed his being
And died,
And wait for a miracle of spring.

If you read Robert Frost or Wang Wei

On your way

To your cottage in late

December, you'll hear mountains meditate.

If you have theories of the snow

In May, try Vermont. Go

Under the crazy full moon, chase a horse

For a frozen lake or two.

Yell his name until you're hoarse

He'll come back on his own. Be alone—maybe a dog

For a friend. Dawning fog

Will walk you up the mountain to a daffodil.

In the mist, eat your fill

And sit down cold and lost

In a pasture with cranky Robert Frost.

Laughing lost in the mountains, I Wang Wei
Took the lone way
Up Deep South Peak. I met
A woodcutter. Next to a stream
We shouted a few words. Then back to dream-
Time in my cottage. I could forget
The Court a while. Beyond the hills a mist
Turned paddies into amethyst.
My heart is terrified of empty rooms. I'll wait,
Singing, for you by my thorn gate.

Poets and bums

Are natural chums.

Our flare

Lies in our agony like Baudelaire.

On the city street

We walk broke, savoring defeat.

Big eyes at night,

Poet and bum, we're baking dreams of light.

Odd?

Why? When we are God.

Ways of Nonsense

Pissing in the forest under an elm,

Connects you to a cosmic realm.

If you pick your nose,
You're not a rose.

The locked heart

Of a pal who never lets a word slip

From the soul's lip

Or never booms a fart

Or even pipes a tiny secret fizz

Leaves no key

Who she or he

Is.

After you're dirty, depressed and demonically

Pee

And dance in the shower,

You're a flower.

Ways of Greece and China

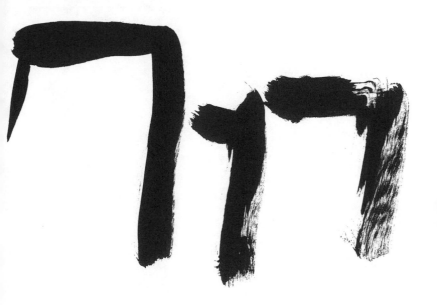

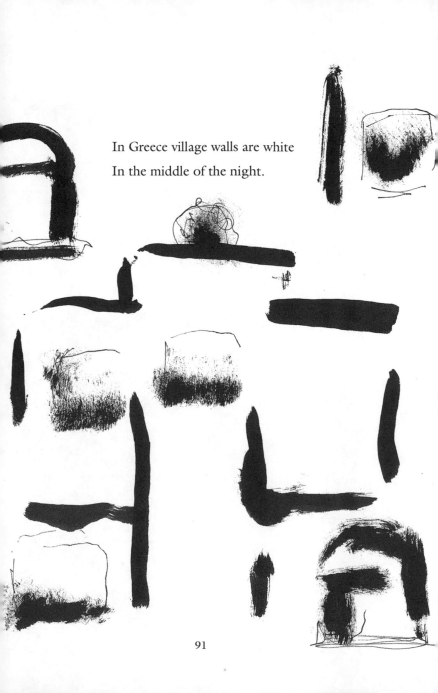

In Greece village walls are white
In the middle of the night.

91

Suddenly in rare
Late afternoon air
Blowing on the island's prickly pear
On Perseus Street,
Bells of death drift down from a Greek
White monastery near the peak.

If you like mountain village time,
Cool like spring marble, climb
With a friend among blue Epirus pines,
Feel the sun, catch the gossip, play
Backgammon half the day
And sip the local turpentines.

For brightness in your soul,
Find a dry hill with wild herbs and stroll.

If life is dark it's also white.

Greek walls of light.

December in a Beijing hutong we
Talked poetry,
Were cold, happy. We knew
Even the secret police had no clue
How unpoor
We were drinking green tea on the floor.

When old Chinese men take their birds
With them and exchange a few words
Near the twilight Forbidden City,
The caged birds feel no self-pity.

Sweating in the Gobi, if you enjoy a melon

Go to white Kashgar in a van,

To the desert pearl of Turkestan

Under the Himalayas. Find a Uighur felon

In the horse market, sit at his table

And share a delicious spit-polished bagel.

Then borrow his market knife

And cut out a drippy slice of life.

Alone in the Gobi an abandoned mosque

Seems to be a white kiosk

Radiating spirit from a stone eye,

A dome built to mystify.

Ways of Being

If you ache
You may wake.

If you soar
Keep a pillow on the floor.

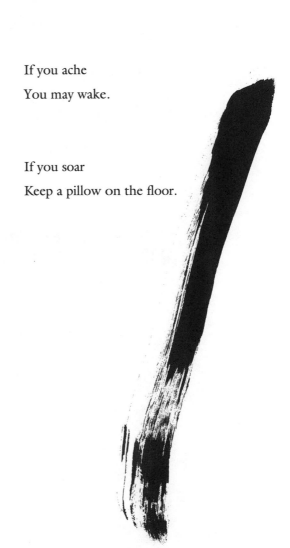

If you look for a violet

In blue Tibet,

Breathe deep but never sigh.

Tibet is very high.

Drink oxygen and fire on your sojourn.

Life is a slow burn.

Lost in the wood

On a narrow way, it's good

To be a wild

And mild child.

Look at the clouds. Fix

A day

To mix

Your heart with that firmament, and cheerfully

Be

On your way.

Around the bend

And in your head you know a civil war,

But in the end

Only you, quiet friend,

Outwit the raging minotaur.

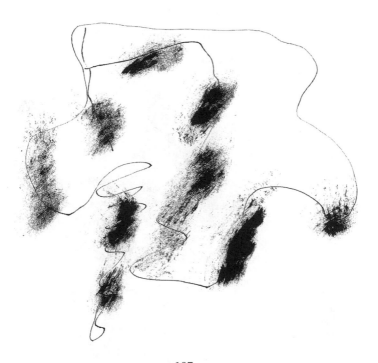

When out of weariness

Or stress

You want to die,

Why?

Look your children or lover in the eye.

If no one yet

Is there, forget

The scorpions a while. It's a mistake

A fatal one, to die. You cannot wake.

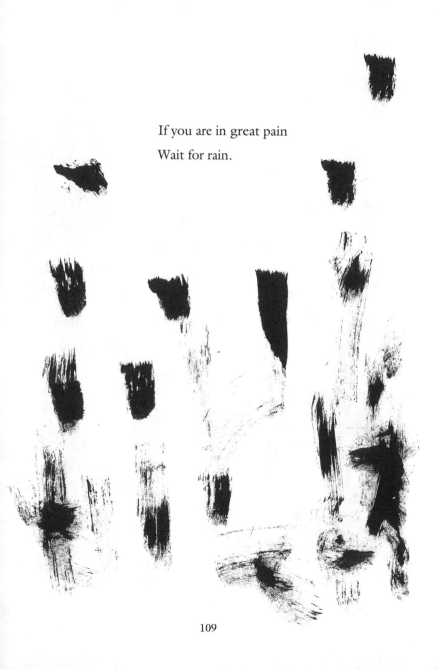

If you are in great pain
Wait for rain.

Wait. A surprise peals in the mud.

Sun in your blood.

It's no fun to be free

In sour eternity.

Although this afternoon you're numb,

I'll come

Or someone. Poison is an ancient way

Of turning into yesterday.

Though late,

You grow from ashes if you wait.

When a dandelion grows enough,

It becomes a see-through puff.

When you're down
A while, ache has a way
Of leaving town.
Joy blunders in—a visionary day
Of Billy Blake
Painting or eating raisin cake.
To be free of black eternity,
Be.

Out of the gloomiest night

Daybreak is white.

If you want this book to end,
Love me and your friend.

Mug to mug,

Hug.

If you're alone,

Don't moan.

Read this and don't be blue.

We're two.

Apology For Funny Ways

Some of the poems and poets I have cared for most have come from odd gnomic sources: fragments from ancient Greek poetry, especially Sappho and Alkaios, whom I translated years ago; the titles of Goya's *Disasters of the War* and his *Caprichos*, which are aphoristic poems at once poignant and the enemy of sentimentality; the *dichos* (sayings) of Sancho Panza; Laotze's *Tao Te Ching*; sayings in modern Greek and Spanish, such as the Greek, "If you've eaten the donkey you might as well eat the tail," or the Spanish, "Dress me slowly, I'm in a hurry," or almost anything that Jorge Luis Borges said in conversation, since, like Sancho Panza, he had the tongue to turn everything into its profound and funny opposite.

In poetry the particular reveals the whole, while in philosophy the concept speaks and with luck reaches the particular. In Chinese, Greek, and Spanish poetry, the image and landscape dominate. I like the feelable landscape always there to retell the soul. Given the agon between singular and abstract, it is strange that I should be attracted to gnomic poetry, to aphorism, which tends to favor idea and concept over object and symbol. Yet gnomic or wisdom verse lies between the utter picture-making of poetry and idea-preaching of philosophy, combining something of both.

In reality I prefer the thing to its verbal sign (and therefore enjoy the visual arts) and would not be unhappy to have John Cage's silent music apply to the poem. Once, decades ago, Cage and I were caught in a blizzard in Connecticut, and through the evening of snow lasting till dawn the composer of four minutes and thirty-three seconds tried to convince me to compose poetry without words; yet, in his gnomic ways, he gave no alternative to speech. And it is true that among the Presocratics and in old Asia, the verb of silence is more eloquent than verbal noise. The *Tao Te Ching* says one who talks doesn't know, one who knows doesn't talk. But why the aphoristic poem? It is also speech.

Having reached a certain age of beginnings — and beginnings is what a life in art gives — I began to feel the need not to separate learned from popular poetry, philosophy from song, the word from an ink drawing. So this form of poetry fell on me, and as the good scribe I recorded it. I tumbled into it, am still surprised, yet always welcome accident and error as the gift of an imperfect godhead in love with art. While perfect truth is impossible — a wishful lie — wisdom untruths are plausible and pleasant, especially when, with word images, paintings, and calligraphy, an old Persian, Japanese, or Chinese utters them in crisp verse. I found that untruths, contradictions, the absolute lies we live by, work very well in brief lines.

Like the Greeks in their elegiac meters, one can be funny, depressed, perfectly thingy yet conceptual, all at once. Often the result is pure idea, but with a stab: "Sometimes in solitude, / The truth is rude." At least the truth is given rude physicality. Here, I am indebted to the Spanish poet of image and idea, of forgetting and oblivion, Antonio Machado, who wrote: *"En mi soledad / he visto cosas muy claras / que no son verdad"* (in my solitude / I've seen very clear things / which are not true). Or, like Emily Dickinson, who makes idea object, as in "Hope fell down the hill," I mix thing and idea: "Drink oxygen and fire on your sojourn. Life is a slow burn."

A sequence of brief Blakean verse has allowed me pathos and irony and humor: "If you ache / You may wake." // "If you soar / Keep a pillow on the floor." Or, "If you are in great pain / Wait for rain." Or provided an occasion to draw with ink, "Out of the gloomiest night / Daybreak is white." Finally, I could be nutty and say, "Mug to mug, / Hug." The aphorism lets me speak of my late brother ("When a brother decides to die / You cry.") and return to the China of Wang Wei and the Gobi, to Greek village walls white in the middle of the night, to Lorca spinning in spearmint weathervanes and lemon spring, and to the Black Squad bullet of his death at Ainadamar, "The Fountain of Tears." It is a Greek or Palatine Anthology opening ways anywhere.

Aphorism has also taken me away from me. There is only one reference to "me" in the book: "If you want this book to end, / Love me and your friend." So this book is for you, the secret lone reader, especially if you feel like joining the cosmos by peeing in the sea or simply walking in the arid hills of the Greek Islands: "For brightness in your soul, / Find a dry hill with wild herbs and stroll."

My Greek wife began as a short-story writer and became a painter. I began as a painter and turned to poetry. One afternoon in my studio on Mount Penteli, a friend came up the stairs, looked at the work on the walls and on my easel, uttered an unfriendly ugh, and I quit. Then, two decades later, in 1972, I began to do ink drawings for my books, beginning with the poems of Mao. In the past I did portraits of seventeenth-century and contemporary Spanish masters of the sonnet and drew the South Mountains of Wang Wei's country poems. Chinese friends flattered me by saying my lines had bones. One early evening — I wish I could remember the trigger — the lyrics in *Funny Ways* incited me to do companion dry-brush ink drawings. I did them all through the night, finishing an hour after dawn. When I sent them to the University Press of New England, I sheepishly asked the designer and editor to select what was best. No, they wanted them all. So came this book of ink and ink.

WILLIS BARNSTONE

UNIVERSITY PRESS OF NEW ENGLAND
publishes books under its own imprint and is the publisher for
Brandeis University Press, Brown University Press, University
of Connecticut, Dartmouth College, Middlebury College
Press, University of New Hampshire, University of Rhode
Island, Tufts University, University of Vermont, and Wesleyan
University Press.

ABOUT THE AUTHOR   Willis Barnstone was born
in Lewiston, Maine, and educated at Bowdoin, Columbia, and
Yale. He has lived and worked in Spain, France, Greece, South
America, and China, including an appointment as Fulbright
Professor of American Literature at Beijing Foreign Studies
University in 1984–85. He has published more than forty
books, including volumes of poetry, criticism, and translations
from Chinese, Spanish, and Greek. He has also collaborated
with his daughter Aliki and his son Tony on anthologies and
translations. A Guggenheim Fellow, NEA and NEH Fellowship
recipient, and two-time Pulitzer Prize nominee, Barnstone is
currently Professor of Comparative Literature and Spanish at
Indiana University.

Library of Congress Cataloging-in-Publication Data
Barnstone, Willis, 1927–
Funny ways of staying alive / Willis Barnstone.
p. cm.   ISBN 0–87451–629–3   I. Title.
PS3503.A6223F8   1993   811'.54—dc20   92-38349
♾